BOBCATS

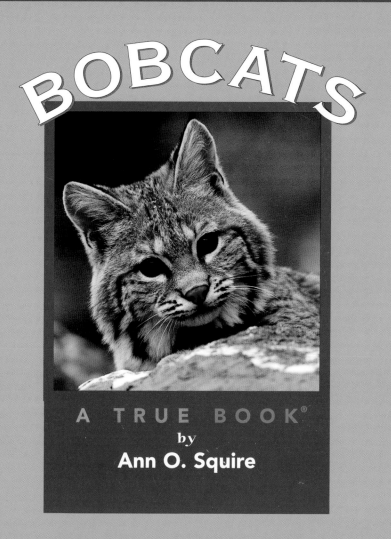

A TRUE BOOK®

by

Ann O. Squire

Children's Press®
A Division of Scholastic Inc.

New York Toronto London Auckland Sydney
Mexico City New Delhi Hong Kong
Danbury, Connecticut

A bobcat perched in a tree

Reading Consultant
Nanci R. Vargus, Ed.D.
Assistant Professor,
School of Education,
University of Indianapolis

Content Consultant
Kathy Carlstead, Ph.D.
Research Scientist,
Honolulu Zoo

Dedication:
For Evan

Library of Congress Cataloging-in-Publication Data

Squire, Ann.
  Bobcats / by Ann O. Squire.
      p. cm. — (A True book)
  Summary: Describes the physical characteristics, habitats, and behavior of bobcats.
  Includes bibliographical references and index.
  ISBN 0-516-22791-2 (lib. bdg.)   0-516-27931-9 (pbk.)
  1. Bobcat—Juvenile literature. [1. Bobcat.] I. Title. II. Series.
QL737.C23S638 2004
599.75'36—dc21
                                              2003005173

CHILDREN'S PRESS, and A TRUE BOOK™, and associated logos are trademarks and or registered trademarks of Scholastic Library Publishing. SCHOLASTIC and associated logos are trademarks and or registered trademarks of Scholastic Inc.

1 2 3 4 5 6 7 8 9 10 R 14 13 12 11 10 09 08 07 06 05

ontents

An American Cat   5

Bobcat Habitats   12

Finding Food   20

Raising Kittens   28

Threats to the Bobcat   38

To Find Out More   44

Important Words   46

Index   47

Meet the Author   48

A bobcat in the Rocky Mountains

An American Cat

When you think about wild cats, what comes to mind? Do you picture a pride of lions snoozing under the African sun? Maybe you imagine a tiger **stalking** its **prey** in the forests of India. If you think that wild cats are found only in far-off lands, think again. North America is home to several kinds of wild cat. The

Bobcats are small compared to most other wild cats.

most common is the bobcat, which lives throughout the western United States and Canada.

The bobcat is one of the smallest wild cats, weighing only 15 to 30 pounds (about 7 to 14 kilograms). That is about as big as a medium-sized dog. A bobcat has black-tufted ears, a spotted coat, and a short, black-tipped tail. The bobcat's markings help it blend into the rocky, forested areas where it lives. Its soft and silky fur ranges in color from pale grey to reddish brown.

Can you spot the bobcat? Its spotted markings help it blend into its surroundings.

The easiest way to recognize a bobcat is by its short tail. Even a full-grown adult bobcat has a tail that is only about 5 inches (13 centimeters) long. It is this short, or "bobbed," tail that gives the bobcat its name.

The bobcat is named for its short, "bobbed" tail.

A bobcat running after prey

Like most other cats, bobcats are solitary. This means that they live alone rather than in groups. Bobcats are carnivores, or meat-eaters, and spend much of their time hunting for prey. A bobcat's sharp eyesight and excellent

A bobcat resting among some thick shrubs

hearing help it hunt at night as well as during the day.

When not hunting, bobcats rest in sheltered spots in caves, hollow logs, or thick shrubs. Female bobcats also use these areas as **dens** when they give birth to kittens.

The Canada Lynx

The Canada lynx, another small wild cat, is a close relative of the bob- cat. Canada lynx usually live farther north than bobcats do. Lynx have some special

A Canada lynx chasing a mouse

adaptations that help them survive in the snow and cold. These include furred footpads, long legs, and large feet that act almost like snowshoes. Because bobcats do not live as far north as Canada lynx do, they do not have these special body features.

Bobcat Habitats

Most of the world's bobcats live in the United States, although they can be found as far north as Canada and as far south as Mexico. Bobcats live in many different kinds of **habitats**, including forests and wooded areas, swamps, mountains, and deserts. Some bobcats even

Bobcats can survive in many habitats, including deserts (left) and forests (below).

Bobcats like to hide behind bushes or tall grasses while hunting their prey.

make their homes near cities.
Bobcats can adapt to nearly any
habitat. If an area has enough

small animals and enough shrubs or trees for a bobcat to hide behind while hunting, there's a good chance that a bobcat can live there.

A bobcat must cover a lot of ground to find enough to eat. Every bobcat has a home range, or territory, in which it lives and hunts. In areas that have are plenty of prey animals, a bobcat's territory can be as small as 1.5 square miles (4 square kilometers). In places

A bobcat spends much of its time hunting for food.

where food is more difficult to find, the bobcat must hunt in a much larger area—sometimes up to 25 square miles (65 sq km). When a territory is very big, a bobcat may find several dens and sleep in a different one each night.

The territories of male and female bobcats sometimes overlap, but female bobcats refuse to share their territories with other females. Bobcats have several ways of showing that a territory is already taken. One of the most obvious markers is a tree scratch. Using its

A bobcat marking its territory by scratching a fallen log

front claws, the bobcat makes long scratch marks in the trunk of a tree, leaving a scent from special **glands** in the paws. Another bobcat passing by can see the scratches and smell the scent of the territory's owner.

A bobcat may also mark its territory by scraping leaves, dirt, and twigs into a pile and then leaving body waste on top of the pile. This smelly marker sends a clear message that the territory is taken.

Finding Food

Bobcats are very active. They spend more than three-fourths of their time **patrolling** their territory and looking for food. They do most of their hunting at dawn and dusk, when rabbits, squirrels, and other small animals may have more difficulty spotting **predators**.

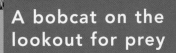

A bobcat on the
lookout for prey

When searching for food, a
bobcat watches for any sign
of movement. It listens for
the rustling noises of small
animals in the **underbrush**.

21

Bobcats stalk their prey silently before attacking (left). When it is close enough to catch its prey, the bobcat pounces (below).

The hairy tufts on the tips of the bobcat's ears act like antennae, helping the cat to hear the slightest sound.

Once the bobcat has spotted prey, it creeps slowly forward. The soft pads on its feet help the bobcat to stalk silently. When it is within 10 feet (3 meters) of its prey, the bobcat pounces. Then it uses its claws to grab the prey. It uses its sharp teeth to bite the animal's neck.

The bobcat hunts some types of prey in a different way. Instead of stalking, the cat finds a hidden spot and waits patiently for a prey animal to come along. This works well for such prey as rabbits, which often hop along the same path again and again. When the unknowing rabbit gets within a few inches of the bobcat's hiding place, the cat leaps out and grabs it.

This bobcat is about to catch a snowshoe hare.

Besides rabbits, bobcats eat squirrels, rats, mice, birds, fish, and many other small animals. They sometimes even catch small deer. A bobcat

A bobcat eating a trout

can eat only about 3 pounds
(1.4 kg) of meat at one time.
If it is lucky enough to capture

an animal that is larger than that, the bobcat will drag the prey away and hide it in a safe spot. Then it will come back several times to feed, eating as much as it can each time.

Since most of their prey animals are small, bobcats must eat a lot of them. Scientists have estimated that a mother bobcat and her three kittens will eat at least 3,800 rats, 3,200 mice, and 700 rabbits in a single year!

Raising Kittens

In late fall or early winter, bobcats get together for mating. For several days, the male and female hunt, eat, and do everything together. After mating, though, the male and female leave one another and return to their solitary lives.

Male and female bobcats come together only at mating time.

A mother bobcat nursing her newborn kittens

After about two months, the female finds a protected den. Here she gives birth to a litter of two or three tiny, helpless kittens. For two months, the kittens stay in hiding, drinking only their mother's milk. After that, the mother begins to bring back solid food for the kittens to eat. When the kittens are about five months old, their mother teaches them how to hunt. She also brings live

A young bobcat kitten with its mother

prey back to the den so that the kittens can learn how to kill with a bite to the neck.

At eight or nine months, the kittens have learned everything their mother can teach them. By this time, the mother has mated again and is pregnant with a new litter. She is eager to have her older kittens leave so that they do not harm the new kittens when they are born. To get rid of them, the mother stops bringing food to the older kittens. She may even chase them out of her territory.

After leaving their mother, the young bobcats some-times hang around on the edge of her territory for a while. Eventually, each one strikes out on its own, looking for an unoccupied area that can become its new territory. If there are few bobcats in the habitat, the young may find unused territories very

Bobcat kittens begin to learn how to hunt when they are a few months old.

A bobcat patrols its territory
along a river in Montana.

near to where they were born. A young bobcat might also take over a territory left empty by the death of another bob-cat. Sometimes, however, a young bobcat must travel more than 100 miles (161 km) before finding a place to call home.

Threats to the Bobcat

Bobcats in the wild have few natural enemies. Occasionally, they are attacked by mountain lions, and coyotes sometimes try to take young kittens. But the greatest threat to the bobcat's survival comes from a much more dangerous predator: humans.

These bobcats were killed so that people could sell their fur.

For hundreds of years, people have trapped bobcats for their beautiful fur. The killing of bobcats increased after it became illegal to kill cheetahs, ocelots, and other spotted cats. Unfortunately, bobcats are not protected in most states.

Another threat to the bob-cat's survival is loss of habitat. As cities grow larger and as forests are cleared to make way for houses, bobcats have fewer and fewer places to live. A bobcat may find that its home range has been cut

As humans take over more and more wilderness land, there are fewer places where bobcats can live.

in half by a superhighway, or that part of its territory has been turned into a shopping mall. Smaller territories mean

A bobcat in Utah's Uinta National Forest

less food. The sad result is that many bobcats will starve.

One way to help the bobcat would be to ban hunting them for fur. Space could be set aside where they can roam free, without the threat of hunters and other human disturbance. If we can do that, these beautiful wild cats will be part of the American land-scape for many years to come.

To Find Out More

Here are some additional resources to help you learn more about bobcats:

Books

Arnold, Caroline. **Bobcats** (Early Bird Nature Books). Lerner Publications, 1997.

Barrett, Jalma. **Bobcat** (Wildcats of North America). Blackbirch Press, 1998.

Hodge, Deborah. **Wild Cats: Cougars, Bobcats, and Lynx.** Kids Can Press, 1999.

Kobalenko, Jerry. **Forest Cats of North America.** Firefly Books Ltd., 1997.

Swinburne, Stephen, R. **Bobcat: North America's Cat.** Boyds Mills Press, 2001.

Organizations and Online Sites

The Bobcat (DesertUSA)

http://www.desertusa.com/ april96/du_bcat.html

Information on the habitats, body features, habits, and life cycle of the bobcat.

Bobcat Ecology

http://www.coryi.org/ bobcatecology.htm

A detailed description of bobcat ecology and behavior from a wildlife foundation that conducts bobcat radio-tracking studies in Florida.

Oakland Zoo: Bobcat

http://www.oaklandzoo.org/ atoz/azbobcat.html

This site includes a fact sheet about the bobcat.

Important Words

adaptations changes that living things have gone through over time so that they fit in better with their environment

dens sleeping places of wild animals

glands organs in the body that either produce natural chemicals or allow substances to leave the body

habitats places where animals or plants naturally live and grow

patrolling traveling around an area to protect it

predators animals that hunt and kill other animals for food

prey animal hunted by other animals

stalking sneaking up on one's prey

underbrush bushes and other plants that grow beneath large trees in the forest

Index

(**Boldface** page numbers
indicate illustrations.)

Canada, 6, 12
Canada lynx, 11, **11**
cheetahs, 40
claws, 19, 23
coat, 7, **7**
coyotes, 38
den, 10, 17, 31, 33
deserts, 12, **13**
ears, 7, 23
eating, 26-27, **26**
eyesight, 9
feet, 11, 23
forests, 12, **13**
fur, 7, 39, 43
habitat, 12, 14, 34, 40
hearing, 10
hunting, 9, **9**, 10, **14**, 15,
    16, **16**, 20, **21**, **22**, 24,
    28, 31, 43
kittens, 10, 27, **30**, 31, **32**,
    33, 34, **35**, 38
marking territory, 17, **18**, 19

mating, 28, **28**
Mexico, 12
mountain lions, 38
mountains, 12
North America, 5
ocelots, 40
pouncing, **22,** 23
predators, 20
prey, 5, 9, 15, 23, 24, 27,
    33
rabbits, 24
Rocky Mountains, **4**
shrubs, 10, **10**
size of bobcats, 6
snowshoe hare, **25**
swamps, 12
tail, 7, 8, **8**
teeth, 23
territory, 15, 17, 19, 20,
    34, **36,** 37, 41
threats to bocats, 38, **39,**
    40, **41,** 43
Uinta National Forest, **42**
United States, 6, 12
wild cats, 5, 6, 43

Meet the Author

Ann O. Squire has a Ph.D. in animal behavior. Before becoming a writer, she spent several years studying African electric fish and the special signals they use to communicate with each other. Dr. Squire is the author of many books on animals and natural-science topics, including *Cheetahs, Lions, African Animals*, and *Animal Homes*. She and her children, Emma and Evan, share their home with a not-so-wild cat named Isabel.

Photographs ©2005: Corbis Images: 4 (W. Perry Conway), 2 (Renee Lynn), 26 (Joe McDonald), 39 (Tim Wright); Dembinsky Photo Assoc.: 18 (Claudia Adams), 7 (Dominique Braud), 13 bottom (Bill Lea), 14 (Jim Roetzel); ImageState/Ron Sanford: cover; Index Stock Imagery/Tim Fitzharris: 9; Masterfile/Tim Fitzharris: 21; Network Aspen/Ricardo Savi: 22 top; Peter Arnold Inc.: 42 (Kevin Schafer), 25 (Jean F. Stoick); Photo Researchers, NY: 22 bottom (Tim Davis), 16 (E.R. Degginger), 1 (Jeff Lepore), 30 (Carolyn A. McKeone), 41 (Blair Seitz), 29 (M.H. Sharp); The Image Works/Tom Brakefield: 11, 32; Viesti Collection, Inc./Robert Winslow: 8, 35; Visuals Unlimited: 6, 36 (Joe McDonald), 10, 13 top (Tom Walker).